PuzzleMania®
Farm Puzzles

HIGHLIGHTS PRESS

Honesdale, Pennsylvania

CONTENTS

When you finish a puzzle, check it off √.
Good luck, and happy puzzling!

Do the Math

A-Mazing!

Hidden Pictures®

Look Twice

Wordplay

Fun & Games

Moo-ve It Along

These five cows have wandered away from their owners. Using the clues below, can you figure out which cow belongs to which rancher?

Moosic

Munch

Cowly

Cuddles

Ferdie

Use the chart to keep track of your answers. Put an **X** in each box that can't be true and an **O** in boxes that match.

	Moosic	Munch	Cowly	Cuddles	Ferdie
Buck					
Jeannie					
Roy					
Sasha					
Tex					

1. Buck's cow is two colors.

2. Jeannie and her cow have the same number of letters in their names.

3. Tex is not fond of longhorns, but he likes bells.

4. Sasha's cow, which does not have horns, is the same color as another cow, but not the same color as Buck's cow.

Illustrated by Dave Clegg   Puzzle by Lori Mortensen

5

Sheep-Shearing Season

It's sheep-shearing season (Can you say that three times fast?), and Dudley and his sheepdog, Zip, are herding their flock to the shearing shed. Can you help them find the way?

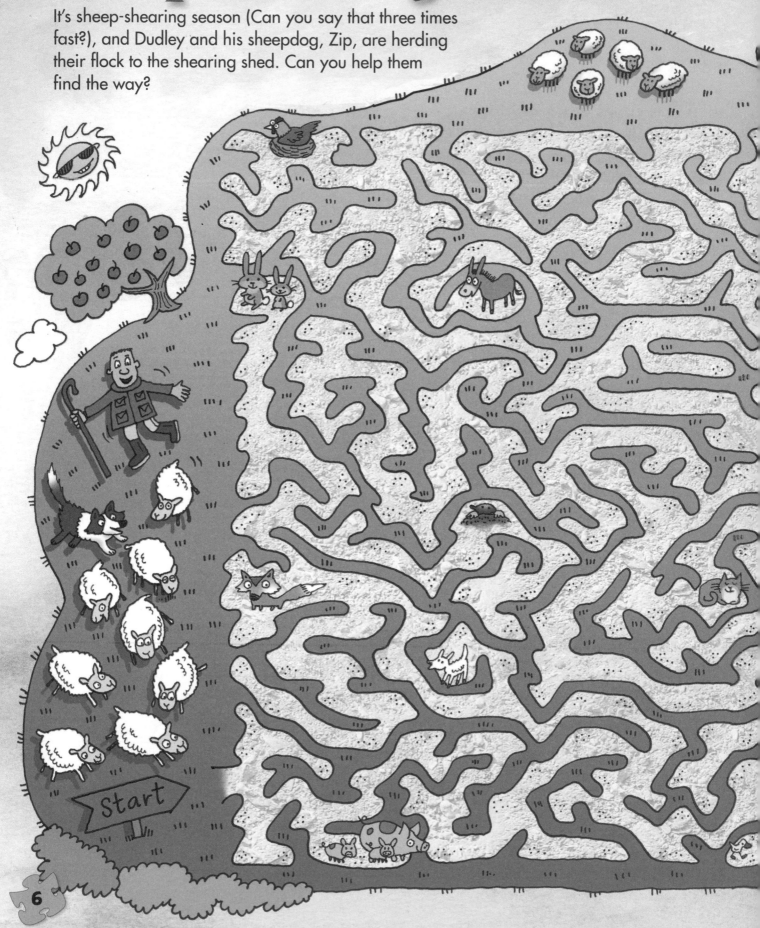

Start

Finish

Illustrated by Beccy Blake

7

Farm Follies

Soo-wee! There are some strange sights on this farm today. Can you find at least **25** odd, weird, or wacky things in this picture?

9

Illustrated by Kevin Rechin

There is more than meets the eye at this pumpkin farm. Can you find the hidden objects?

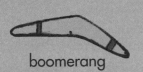
boomerang

pennant

ring

fishhook

rake

canoe

umbrella

paper clip

open book

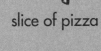
slice of pizza

feather

comb

envelope

key

mitten

megaphone

fish

ruler

kite

football

banana

mug

crown

11

Roundabout

To solve this riddle, start at the arrow. Then count around the wheel to **every third letter**, writing those letters in order in the spaces below. Keep going until you've been to each letter exactly once. We've done the first two letters to get you started. If you're not chicken, you'll scratch out the answer in no time.

Why did the chicken cross the water park?

T O _ _ _ _ _ _ _

_ _ _ _ _ _ _ _ _

_ _ _ _ _ _

Letters around the wheel: T T R O H S G E L E O I T T D T H E O E

Illustrated by Carolina Farias

Tic Tac Row

Each of these horses has something in common with the other two horses in the same row. For example, in the first row across, all three horses have spots. Look at the other rows across, down, and diagonally. Can you tell what's alike in each row?

Illustrated by Carolina Farias

Word for Words

The letters in **BASKETBALL** can be used to make many other words. Use the clues below to come up with some of them. A nighttime creature, for example, might make you think of the word **BAT**. See how many of the others you can guess.

B A S K E T B A L L

1. A nighttime creature — B A T
2. Drink it iced or hot. — _ _ _
3. Pose a question. — _ _ _
4. First, second, or third — _ _ _ _ _
5. Opposite of short — _ _ _ _
6. Pepper's partner — _ _ _ _
7. To put cookies in the oven — _ _ _ _
8. Not early — _ _ _ _
9. The B in BFF — _ _ _ _
10. Huron or Erie — _ _ _ _
11. Direction of a sunrise — _ _ _ _
12. To Rollerblade — _ _ _ _ _
13. Opposite of most — _ _ _ _ _
14. A horse's home — _ _ _ _ _ _
15. *The Nutcracker* is one. — _ _ _ _ _ _

Hidden Pictures®
Farm Fresh

shoe

artist's brush

cracker

candle

worm

airplane

seashell

slice of bread

15

Illustrated by Mary Sullivan

EGGS FOR SALE

Come and Get It!

These cowboys are cooking up some fun, and you can join them. To learn the answer to this riddle, read each clue to find out what letter goes in each numbered space. Ready? Saddle up!

1. Look on a saddle for this letter.
2. This letter is in the frying pan.
3. You'll find this letter on some spurs.
4. This letter is between two horns.
5. A prairie dog has this letter.
6. Look on a hat for this letter.
7. This letter is in the fire.
8. A coyote is howling at this letter.
9. Look for this letter on a boot.
10. This letter is floating in a pot of water.
11. A lasso is rounding up this letter.
12. This letter is on a rock.

Puzzle by Lori Mortensen

Illustrated by Peter Grosshauser

What do cowboys put on their pancakes?

◯ ◯ ◯ ◯ ◯   ◯ ◯ ◯ ◯ ◯ ◯ ◯
11 4 9 7 2   10 1 12 5 8 6 3

Good Morning

Rise and shine! We've flipped **21** breakfast foods into this grid. Look for them up, down, across, backwards, and diagonally. Now rub the sleep from your eyes and dig in.

Word List

- ~~BACON~~
- BAGEL
- BANANA
- CEREAL
- CROISSANT
- DANISH
- FRIED EGGS
- GRANOLA
- GRAPEFRUIT
- GRITS
- HAM
- HASH BROWNS
- OATMEAL
- OMELET
- PANCAKES
- SAUSAGE
- SCRAMBLED EGGS
- SMOOTHIE
- TOAST
- WAFFLES
- YOGURT

```
        B H B G Q
      H A N A N A B
      V A H K G M C D K
    R N S L A E M T A O Q
    K E E H O S L G T N T D F
    A N I B M G G C R I N J R
  W L N H R E G I E U S A J I H
  K O I T O L E W R G H S S E C
  D N D O W E D F E O P S E D N
 (B A C O N) T E J A Y A I L E U
  E R R M S P L Q L K N O F G L
  G P S A V B X T C C R F G G
  M A R D L M H O A A C A S
    G S T O A S T N K M W
    E U G R I T S E A
    D A C Q V A S
      S S E A T
```

18

Crop Circles

A strange pattern has appeared in Farmer Brown's field. Can you follow the path from START to FINISH?

START

FINISH

Illustrated by Charles Jordan

19

Veggie Q's

To Market, to Market

Help Ellie reach the farmers' market before it closes.

Start

Finish

Illustrated by Mike Moran

Veggies or Not?

Each pair of words has one veggie and one phony. Circle the veggies.

Kale or **Yale?**

Swedish Bard or **Swiss Chard?**

Fennel or **Funnel?**

Oprah or **Okra?**

Jalapeño or **Jalopy?**

Wallaby or **Kohlrabi?**

Vegetable Soup

This bowl is swimming with veggies! Put together the parts to make the names of 4 vegetables.

ROOM   EGG   PUMP   CAR

KIN   ROT   MUSH   PLANT

_____

_____

_____

_____

Hidden Veggies

A vegetable is hidden in the letters of each sentence. Find **Y-A-M** in order in the first sentence. Then find a different veggie in each of the others.

Please try a marshmallow.

Could this be any sillier?

This décor needs to be updated.

An antelope ambled by.

That bee tried to sting me!

Match Up

Can you find four differences between these two baskets?

Far-out Food

On the planet Verdura the aliens who live there look a little like veggies. Can you add a face and other features to this picture to show someone from Verdura?

Horseplay

There were six stalls in this barn, built from thirteen equal sections of wall. Yesterday, one of the horses kicked one wall down. Now the owner of the barn wants to use the remaining twelve walls to form six new stalls of equal size. Can you help? Hint: This one's tricky! You'll need to try a completely different shape than the rectangles used here. Try using toothpicks for the twelve walls, moving them around until you find the answer.

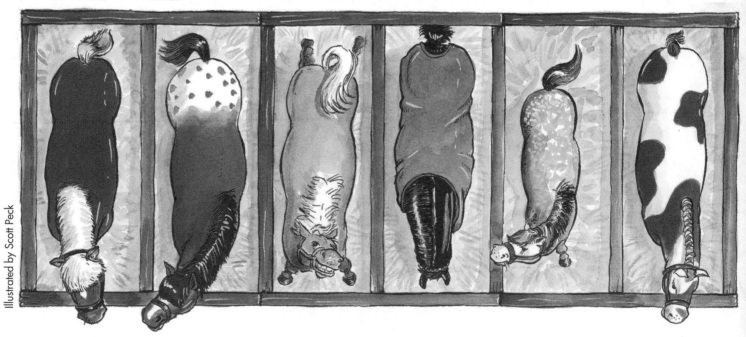

Illustrated by Scott Peck

Hop To It!

Find a path from START to FINISH by hopping from frog to frog. The correct path uses frogs that are juggling an **even number of objects**.

Which objects start with the letter *P*?

START

Find the two matching frogs.

How many objects are being juggled along the right path? Add 'em up!

FINISH

Illustrated by Bonnie Leick

23

GooFy GardeNS

How many silly things can you find in this picture?

Illustrated by Mike Dammer

Garden High Jinks

That Grow Big potion really worked! What do you think
Greer grew in her garden? The world's tallest cornstalk?
A giant dandelion? Or maybe it's a tree that grows
chocolate cupcakes! Draw what you think Greer grew.

Illustrated by Mike Moran

Swing Your Partner

This hoedown is in full swing, but Cowboy Mike can't find his date! Help him find a path on the dance floor.

START

FINISH

Box Drops

Each of these grids contains a farm joke and its punchline. To read the jokes, move the letters up into the boxes directly above them, staying in the same row. But watch out: the letters don't go in the boxes in the same order as they appear.

1

W	H	A	T			D	O					
						?						

		L			E					
K	~~A~~ ~~T~~			E				S	
~~A~~ H	A	P	O	~~D~~ ~~O~~			C	O	O	P
W	H	A	T	L	R	K		Y	H	U	G
T	C	A	R	A	T	D	O	E	P	I	A

2

W	H	A	T			I	S		'			
									?			

		N					L				
	O	~~A~~	A				L				
	O H	A	I	N	E	~~L~~ ~~I~~ N	G			
M	V	P	R	I	C	T	W	~~S~~	S		
F	A ~~W~~	O	A	~~T~~	T	O	I	I	S	A	

The Plot Thickens

Jack and three friends are sharing a plot in their community garden this summer. From the clues below, can you figure out which friend planted what type of veggie and what kind of flower?

Use the chart to keep track of your answers. Put an **X** in each box that can't be true and an **O** in boxes that match.

	Peas	Corn	Squash	Lettuce	Sunflowers	Marigolds	Petunias	Zinnias
Jack								
Lily								
Garrett								
Rosemary								

1. Lily's vegetable and flower start with consecutive letters of the alphabet.

2. Jack does not like corn.

3. Rosemary's veggie and flower start with the same letter.

4. Garrett planted his favorite flowers, petunias.

Puzzle by Karen Smith

Farm Market

Illustrated by Rocky Fuller

Can you find the hidden objects?
When you finish, you can color in the rest of the scene.

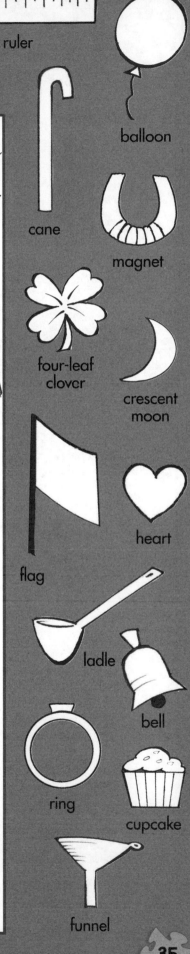

ruler

balloon

cane

magnet

four-leaf clover

crescent moon

flag

heart

ladle

bell

ring

cupcake

funnel

WIGGLE PICTURES

**These farm animals have been twisted and turned.
Can you figure out what each one is?**

Tic Tac Row

Each of these cows has something in common with the other two cows in the same row. For example, in the first row across, all three cows have two horns. Look at the other rows across, down, and diagonally. Can you tell what's alike in each row?

Illustrated by Don Robison

38

Down Under

We're taking this puzzle underground. Twenty-four kinds of foods that grow underground are hidden in this grid. Look for them up, down, across, backwards, and diagonally. Time to dig in!

Illustrated by Hey Kids!

Word List

~~ARROWROOT~~	GINGER	RADISH
BEET	GINSENG	RUTABAGA
CARROT	JICAMA	SCALLION
CASSAVA	KAVA	SHALLOT
CELERIAC	ONION	TARO
CHICORY	PARSNIP	TURNIP
DAIKON	PEANUT	WASABI
GARLIC	POTATO	YAM

```
D A I K O N X P I N R U T
D I R T S C A L L I O N R
P E A N U T R G A R L I C
W O R M A A J A M K A V A
C J N R D D O W A S A B I
A K O I F Y T C C P R C R
S C S S E N A S I A E A E
S H A L L O T M J R G R L
A R R O W R O O T S N R E
V S O I L T P C M N I O C
A Q L L G N E S N I G T T
C H I C O R Y E V P M U D
O N I O N A G A B A T U R
```

Roping Roundup

It's Beginner Roping Day down at the ranch. Each newbie has roped something. But what? Follow the ropes to see what each wrangler has snared.

Illustrated by Jim Paillot

Turtle Crossing

This puzzle is crawling with **27** kinds of turtles. Their names can fit into the grid in just one way. Use the number of letters in each name to figure out where each one belongs. Write in each name and cross it off the list as you go. No hurry. Take your time.

Word List

3 Letters
BOG
BOX
MAP

4 Letters
MUSK
WOOD

5 Letters
BLACK
GREEN

7 Letters
PAINTED
SPOTTED

8 Letters
FALSE MAP
FLATBACK
SNAPPING
STINKPOT
TERRAPIN

9 Letters
BLANDING'S
HAWKSBILL
YELLOW MUD

10 Letters
EASTERN MUD
~~LOGGERHEAD~~
POND SLIDER

11 Letters
KEMP'S RIDLEY
LEATHERBACK
OLIVE RIDLEY
RIVER COOTER

14 Letters
RED-EARED SLIDER
SPINY SOFTSHELL

15 Letters
SMOOTH SOFTSHELL

XING

SLOW

LOGGERHEAD

Illustrated by Brian White

PLANTING ROWS

Read the clues and fill in the words. To get the second clue, remove one letter from CARROTS and rearrange the remaining letters to find the third word. Do the same for the fourth, then the fifth, sixth, and seventh. From the eighth clue on, add a new letter and rearrange the letters for the next word.

CLUES
1. A rabbit's favorite bunch of vegetables
2. Person in a play or film who acts along with the star
3. Way to cook meat
4. Heavenly object, like the sun
5. Sticky black substance
6. In the location of
7. First vowel in the alphabet
8. Indefinite article
9. Old horse
10. Pressed the doorbell
11. Liver, lung, or musical instrument
12. Moans in pain
13. Citrus fruits

1. C A R R O T S

Illustrated by Ben Mahan

44

Tenth Time

This board is marked off in ten equal sections. Each section is lettered. To solve the riddle, check the fractions below each blank. That will tell you which fraction of the board to look at for the correct letter, going from left to right.

A C E I N O P R S T

What did the sign on the chicken coop say?

$\dfrac{8}{10}$ $\dfrac{6}{10}$ $\dfrac{6}{10}$ $\dfrac{9}{10}$ $\dfrac{10}{10}$ $\dfrac{4}{10}$ $\dfrac{5}{10}$ $\dfrac{7}{10}$ $\dfrac{3}{10}$ $\dfrac{1}{10}$ $\dfrac{2}{10}$ $\dfrac{3}{10}$

Illustrated by David Helton

45

chef's hat

flashlight

paintbrush

paper clip

comb

ice-cream cone

toothbrush

baseball bat

mitten

Farmer, Farmer, Shear the Sheep

By Mandy C. Yates

Farmer, Farmer, shear the sheep.
How much wool will you keep?
Just enough to fill the barn,
Then we'll spin it into yarn!

Illustrated by Dave Klug

Double Market

The farmers' market is busy today! See if you can pick out the 12 differences between these pictures.

Illustrated by Mike Dammer

COME AND PLAY

By Dale Cross Purvis

One little pink pig
is sleeping in the sun.
All the other piggies
are having tons of fun.

"Come and play with us!"
the merry piggies say.
But one little pink pig
is sleeping late today!

How many *P's* do you see?

PINK LEMONADE

Well, Hello!

bat

heart

goose

glove

hat

sailboat

tweezers

Illustrated by Tim Davis

hanger

fish

bell

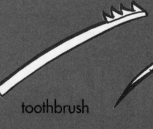
toothbrush

rat

Hello, Yellow!

Fourteen yellow items will fit into this grid. They can fit in just one way. Use the number of letters in each word as a clue to where it should go. Ready? Time to go for the gold— yellow gold, that is!

Word List

~~BEE~~
SUN
CORN
TAXI
CHICK
LEMON
BANANA
BUTTER
CANARY
OMELET
DAFFODIL
GOLDFINCH
SCHOOL BUS
GRAPEFRUIT

WOUND-UP ROUNDUP

How many silly things can you find in this picture?

Illustrated by Chuck Dillon

54

Step by Step

Cowabunga! Follow these steps to draw a cow.

1.

2.

3.

4.

5.

Illustrated by Ron Zalme

Market Time

Tomorrow is the town market, and these tractors must bring their loads back to the barn. Follow each path to see which tractor is pulling which crop.

57

WIGGLE PICTURES

**These yummy fruits have been twisted and turned.
Can you figure out what each one is?**

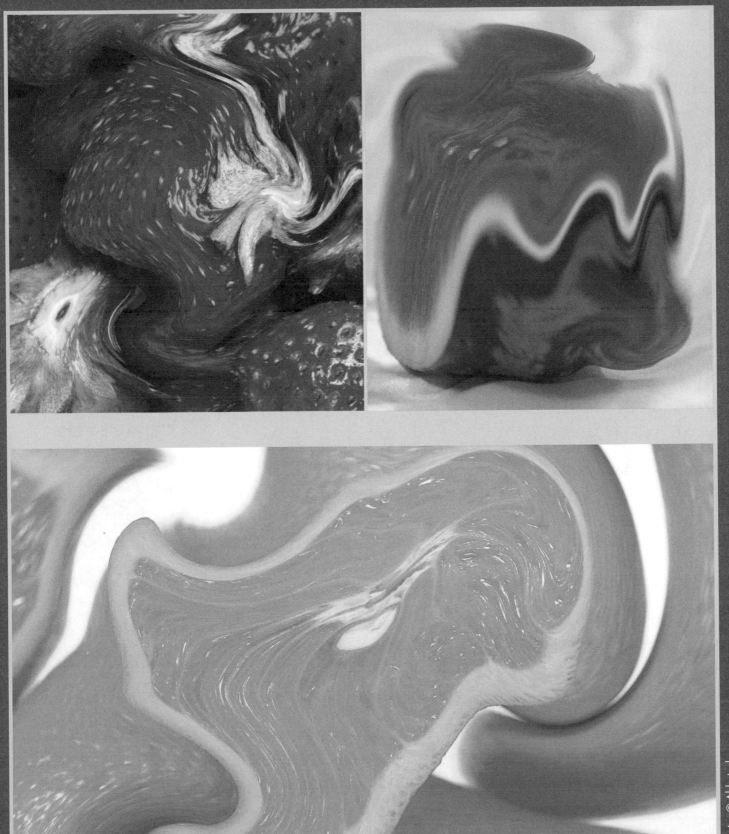

Photos © Ablestock

Big Machines

Time to get to work! We've hidden **18** kinds of farm equipment in the grid. Look for them up, down, across, backwards, and diagonally. See if you can spot them all.

```
S O I L F I N I S H E R A U I R R
S K I D L O A D E R E A I S R E C
K W Y R U L O B P Y S H L E D B U
H M D R A B C A N E Z L K A R A L
S P F P C K T L R Q I C E O E C T
Q D T O F Q E E P R I R T Y P K I
V L I F R Y H R D P P C I K L H V
T S Q Q U S T D N S A L S G O O A
T I L L E R E O T R S W S F W E T
D H V R P E T S T O W V B P H R O
I V H L S T A J L X L M O B E W R
A T G U O C T X A M E Y P P B K F
L M K C D T R A N S P L A N T E R
U C D A T G Q T G I V E M E U A G
S T O N E P I C K E R T U L I K H
K R C O N V E Y O R B E L T B U N
B C O M B I N E H A R V E S T E R
```

Word List

BACKHOE
~~BALER~~
BROADCAST SPREADER
COMBINE HARVESTER
CONVEYOR BELT
COTTON PICKER
CULTIVATOR
PLOW
RAKE
REAPER
SEED DRILL
SKID LOADER
SOIL FINISHER
STONE PICKER
THRESHER
TILLER
TRACTOR
TRANSPLANTER

The Mane Route

Move 1 space down

Move 1 space up

Move 1 space right

Move 1 space left

Brady and his trusty horse, Heywood, are heading back to the stable. Can you help them find the right trail? The symbols will tell you which way to move.

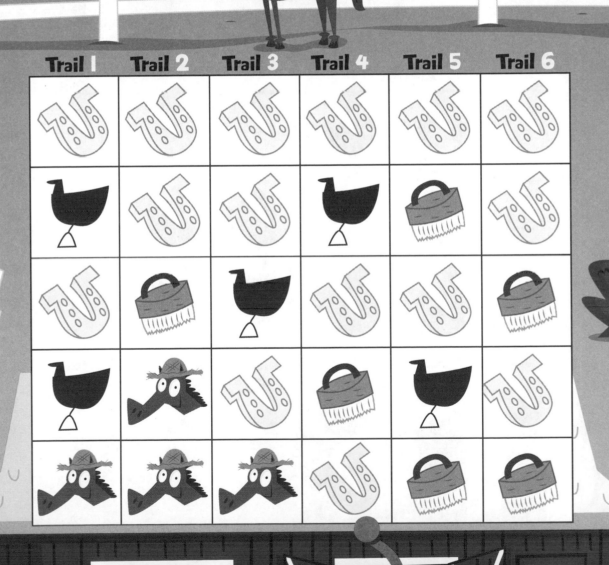

Trail 1   Trail 2   Trail 3   Trail 4   Trail 5   Trail 6

61

Horsing Around

Each horse has one that looks exactly like it. Can you find all the matching pairs? *Giddyup!*

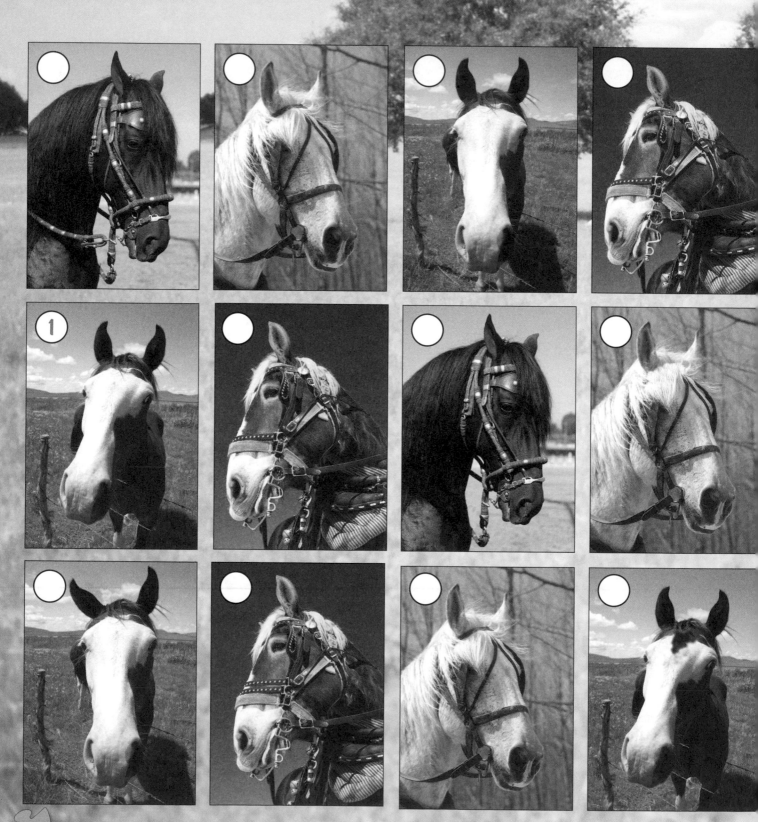

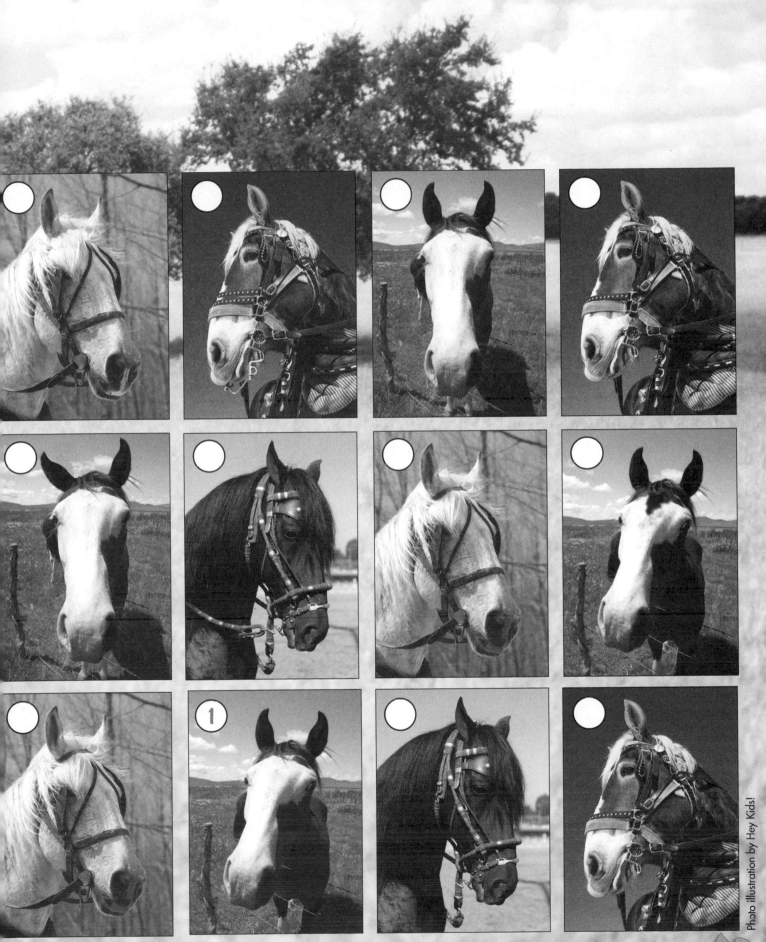

Ah-choo!

Where do sick cows and pigs buy their medicine? To find out, follow the directions below. Each sentence will tell you where one letter is in the grid. Once you've found it, write it in the correct space below the riddle. Got it? Now get a moo-ve on.

1. This letter is the first consonant in the bottom row.
2. Find the letter directly above the **X**.
3. This letter appears three times in the second row.
4. This letter is between two **G**'s.
5. This letter appears twice, side by side, in the same row.
6. Find the letter in between a **J** and an **O**.
7. Count two below the **Q** for this letter.
8. This letter is in the center of the bottom row.
9. Find the letter that is directly below the **Z**.
10. This letter appears in two of the four corners.

F	J	M	O	P	H	A
V	R	E	R	N	R	X
I	Y	Y	C	F	Q	N
S	D	B	G	E	G	K
Y	Z	V	O	K	H	R
E	A	T	C	F	N	F

Where do sick cows and pigs buy their medicine?

$\frac{T}{1} \frac{}{7} \frac{}{4} \quad \frac{}{10} \frac{}{9} \frac{}{3} \frac{}{6} - \frac{}{2} \frac{}{8} \frac{}{5}$

Illustrated by Kelly Kennedy   Puzzle by Sarah Greco

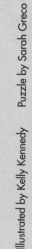

Farm-tastic

Five farm animals are hidden here. Solve the math problems. Then find each equation number in a box. Put the letter from the same box in the blank below the number. See if you can find the names of all five animals by feeding time.

1. 5 + __ = 14

___ ___ ___

2. 7 + 8 = __

___ ___ ___

3. 13 − __ = 3

___ ___ ___

4. __ − 11 = 1

___ ___ ___

5. 2 + 4 = __

___ ___ ___

1 G	2 R	3 T
4 A	5 C	6 M
7 P	8 I	9 O
10 A	11 O	12 D
13 C	14 W	15 G

Digit Does It

Ah, there's nothing more pleasurable to Inspector Digit than working in his garden. But on this sunny afternoon, he was presented with a problem. His neighbor played a trick by planting

Illustrated by John Nez

some phony flowers around the yard. Can you help the inspector dig up some clues and decipher the neighbor's note? The first three words of the letter are **"Dear Inspector Digit."**

Illustrated by Valeri Gorbachev

68

Tiger is headed to town with a tractor full of fresh hay. Can you find the 10 hidden objects that begin with *T*?

tweezers

trombone

trowel

teacup

toothbrush

teapot

tack

telephone

turtle

GOOSE CROSSING

Why did the goose cross the bridge? To find out, use the alphabet code to cross the puzzle bridge below. Start at the letter *T* in the bridge. Then follow that arrow to the next one. To get your code letter, count backwards 5 letters in the alphabet from T. Your next letter is O. Write that letter in the answer space. Keep going counting forwards (+) and backwards (−) from each letter to get to the next one.

ABCDEFGHIJKLMNOPQRSTUVWXYZ

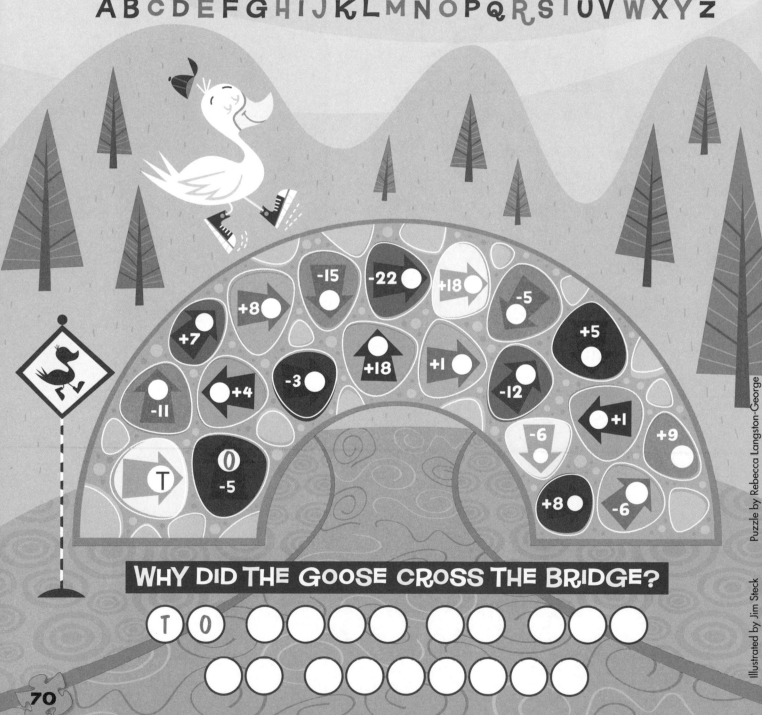

WHY DID THE GOOSE CROSS THE BRIDGE?

T O ◯ ◯ ◯ ◯ ◯ ◯ ◯ ◯ ◯ ◯

◯ ◯ ◯ ◯ ◯ ◯ ◯ ◯

70

Orange Zest

Twenty shades of orange can squeeze into this puzzle. Each will fit in the grid in only one way. Use the number of letters in each word as a clue to where it might fit. "Orange" you glad we filled in one to get you started?

4 Letters
~~RUST~~

5 Letters
AMBER
BLAZE
BURNT
CORAL
FLAME
PEACH
TAWNY

6 Letters
CARROT
SAFETY
SALMON

7 Letters
APRICOT
PERSIAN
PUMPKIN

9 Letters
CHAMPAGNE
ORANGE-RED
PERSIMMON
TANGERINE

10 Letters
ORANGE PEEL
TERRA COTTA

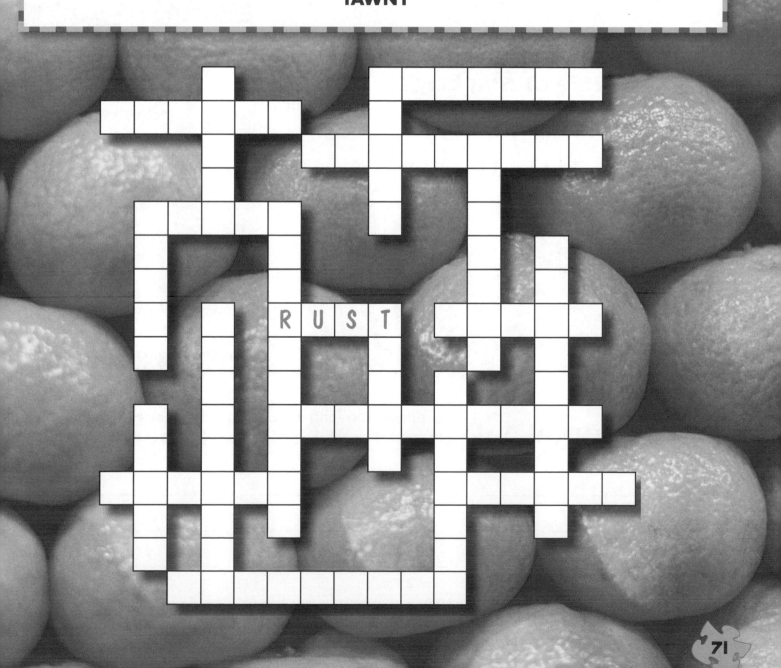

Horse Q's

Horse or Not?

Each pair of words has one horse and one faker. Circle the horses.

Appaloosa or Apple crisp?

Hay bale or Clydesdale?

Palomino or Domino?

Muzzle or Mustang?

Arabian or Caribbean?

Morning or Morgan?

Changing Horses

These pictures may look alike, but take a closer peek. Can you spot five differences between the two pictures?

On Horseback

Equestrian is a long word for a horseback rider. Can you make at least **15** words from the letters in **EQUESTRIAN**?

_____ _____ _____

_____ _____ _____

_____ _____ _____

_____ _____ _____

Horse Talk

Here are six horse sayings and their definitions. Can you guess which are true (**T**) and which are false (**F**)?

1. If someone tells you to **hold your horses**, they want you to wait. **T F**

2. A **dark horse** is someone who is very fashionable. **T F**

3. If information comes **straight from the horse's mouth**, it's probably false. **T F**

4. To **horse around** is to have fun with friends. **T F**

5. Someone who has **horse sense** uses good judgment. **T F**

6. A **one-horse town** is a large, lively city. **T F**

Going Buggy
Which horse is leading this cart?
Illustrated by Mike Moran

Horse Hee-Haw
Fill in the speech bubble!

Puzzles by Carly Schuna

73

Pen Pals

Francine is trying to raise some chickens for a 4-H project. She needs to enclose each rooster with three hens. She has enough material to make just two straight fences inside the pen. Can you help her put the fences in the right place to make four pens, each with one rooster and three hens?

Illustrated by David Helton

Hidden Pictures®
Moo-ving On By

flashlight

key

boot

whistle

broom

hammer

carrot

apple

slice
of cake

Illustrated by R. Michael Palan

spatula

bird

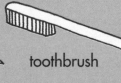
toothbrush

seal

artist's brush

slice of pie

ice-cream
scoop

crayon

75

How many silly things can you find in this picture?

Illustrated by David Helton.

Word for Words

The letters in **DRAGONFLIES** can be used to make many other words. Use the clues below to come up with some of them. A fox's home, for example, might make you think of the word **DEN**. See how many of the others you can guess.

Dragonflies

1. A fox's home   D E N

2. Lassie or Snoopy   __ __ __

3. An American flag color   __ __ __ __

4. Dirt for planting   __ __ __ __ __

5. A __ __ __ __ __ of bread

6. The highest Olympic medal   __ __ __ __ __

7. Hole-in-one sport   __ __ __ __ __

8. A baby horse   __ __ __ __ __

9. They go with a burger   __ __ __ __ __ __

10. A place to grow vegetables   __ __ __ __ __ __

11. A kind of fruit or a bright color   __ __ __ __ __ __

12. Fuel for a car   __ __ __ __ __ __ __ __

Illustrated by Carolina Farias

WIGGLE PICTURES

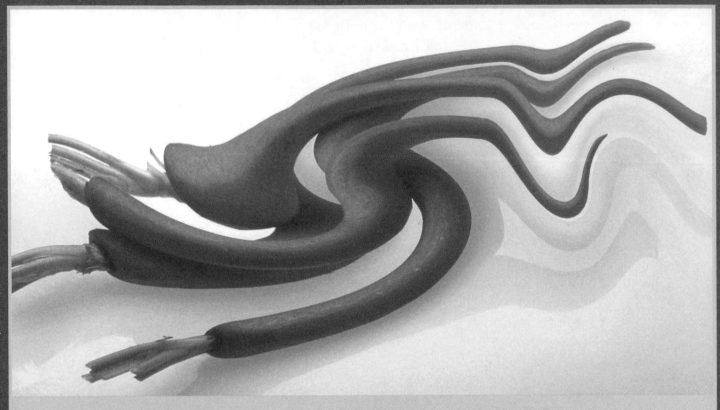

These pictures of vegetables have been twisted and turned. Can you figure out what each one is?

Hay Day

It's haying season, and this farmer and his family have to get the hay bales back to the barn. See if you can find a path.

START

FiNiSH!

Fresh Picked

1

2

3

Which of these puzzle pieces belong in the numbered spaces?

A.

B.

C.

D.

E.

F.

Challenge: Find where the other puzzle pieces belong.

82

Easy as Pie!

Seventeen types of pie are baked into this grid. They are hidden up, down, across, backwards, and diagonally. Go ahead and dig in!

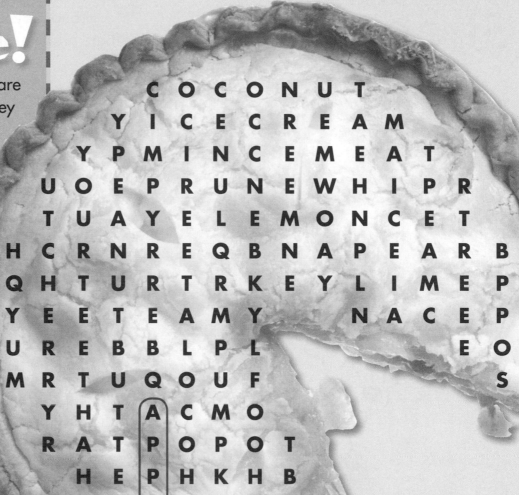

```
      C O C O N U T
      Y I C E C R E A M
    Y P M I N C E M E A T
    U O E P R U N E W H I P R
    T U A Y E L E M O N C E T
  H C R N R E Q B N A P E A R B
  Q H T U R T R K E Y L I M E P
  Y E E T E A M Y   N A C E P
  U R E B B L P L         E O
  M R T U Q O U F         S
  Y H T A C M O
  R A T P O P O T
  H E P H K H B
  R L C I S L
      E A N E X
```

Word List

APPLE

BERRY
CHERRY
CHOCOLATE
COCONUT
ICE CREAM
KEY LIME
LEMON
MINCEMEAT
PEACH
PEANUT BUTTER
PEAR
PECAN
PRUNE WHIP
PUMPKIN
RHUBARB
SHOOFLY

BONUS PUZZLE

When you've circled all the words, we've got an extra treat for you. The answer to the riddle below is hidden in a row or column. See if you can find it.

What's the best thing to put in a pie?

Y __ __ __ __   __ __ __ __!

Puzzle by Stacey Williams

83

Counting Sheep

Can you help Bo Peep find all the groups of similar sheep? (Sheep from the same group may face different directions.) There are five different groups of similar sheep and one unique sheep all by herself.

84

Hidden Pictures®
Tractor Trouble

Can you find these 8 hidden objects in the big picture?

cupcake

dog bone

pencil

glove

comb

eyeglasses

apple

sock

Dot to Dot

Connect the dots from 1 to 19 to
see who else lives on a farm.

Illustrated by David Coulson

Jump On In!

The big race is about to start. Follow each frog's path to find out where each happy hopper finishes in the race. Once you've done that, write the letters from the path of the frog who got first place in order in the spaces below. They will spell the answer to the riddle. Now hop to it!

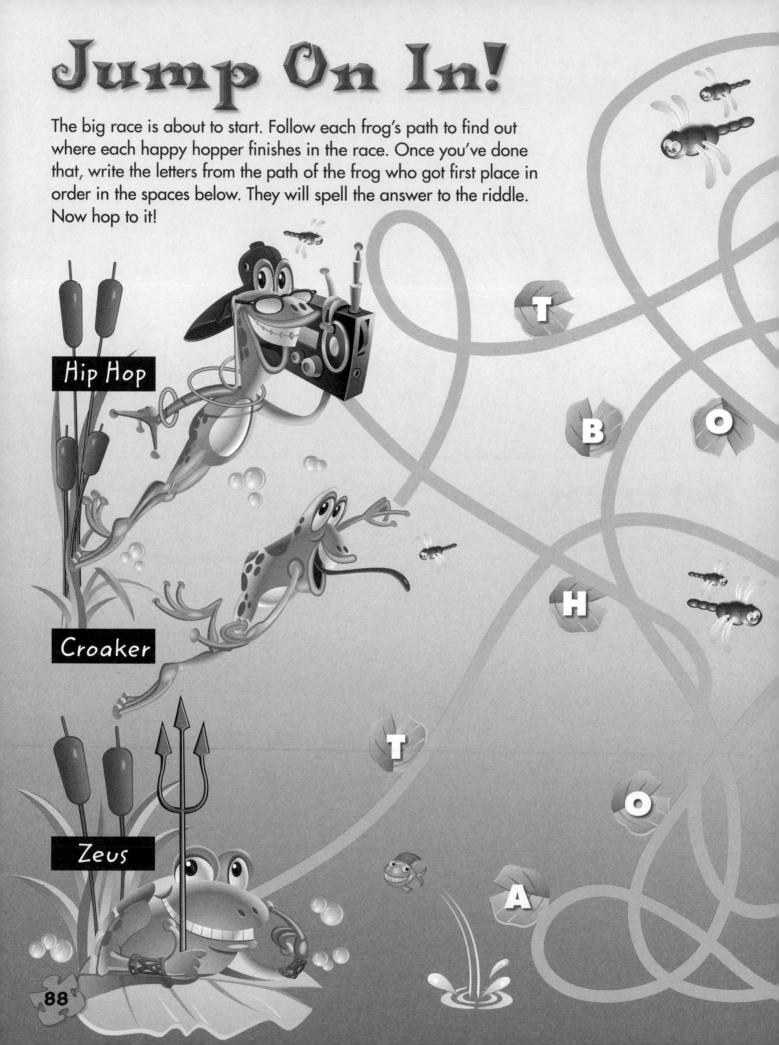

Hip Hop

Croaker

Zeus

T   B   O   H   T   O   A

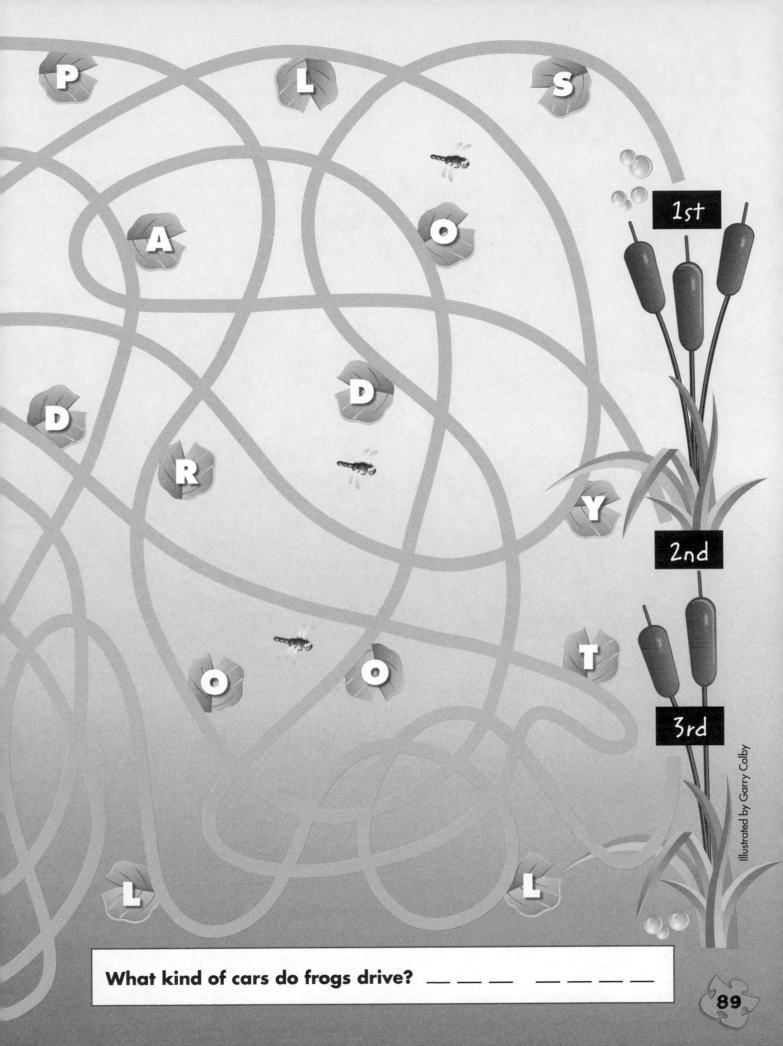

What kind of cars do frogs drive? __ __ __ __ __ __ __ __

89

Illustrated by Garry Colby

Loop-the-Loop

Every number can be looped together with one other number. The key to finding the pairs is to look for those numbers that have a difference of 9 when the smaller number is subtracted from the larger. Pairs can be looped across, up, down, backwards, or diagonally. Each number will be looped with only one other number.

65	57	66	98	107	100
58	74	72	108	87	91
49	81	80	89	99	78
105	67	75	101	110	68
76	96	84	94	102	77
83	92	103	95	86	93

Illustrated by Scott Peck

90

As Fun as a Cow?

We've mixed up a bunch of similes. Similes are phrases that compare two things, as in this sentence: You'll be **as proud as a peacock** if you can figure out all of these! Write the correct word or words on the blank space beside each simile.

1. As brave as A FEATHER _____A LION_____

2. As wise as AN OX _____

3. As light as A WHISTLE _____

4. As silly as PIE _____

5. As solid as A WOLF _____

6. As sharp as A WINK _____

7. As clean as A MULE _____

8. As easy as A FIDDLE _____

9. As fit as A GOOSE _____

10. As free as A PIN _____

11. As stubborn as ~~A LION~~ _____

12. As hungry as A BIRD _____

13. As neat as A ROCK _____

14. As strong as AN ARROW _____

15. As quick as A TACK _____

16. As straight as AN OWL _____

Illustrated by Dan McGeehan

91

Horse Hide

There's more than meets the eye on this riding trail. Can you find the hidden objects?

button

boomerang

comb

envelope

dove

fish

paper clip

sailboat

fishhook

cupcake

pencil

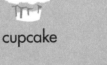
iron   spatula   banana

canoe

high-heeled shoe

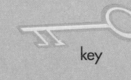
baseball bat

book

spoon

key

slice of watermelon

yo-yo

93

Double Dance

One-step, two-step, three-step! See if you can pick out the 12 differences between these two pictures.

Illustrated by John Courtney

Fences and Fields

pencil

fish

candle

slice of pie

rabbit

fork

banana

teacup

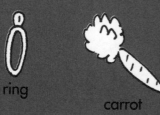

ring

carrot

ice-cream cone

key

comb

nail

tack

Illustrated by Ron Lieser

96

Letter Drop

Only six of the letters in the top line will work their way through this maze to land in the numbered squares at the bottom. When they get there, they will spell out the answer to the riddle.

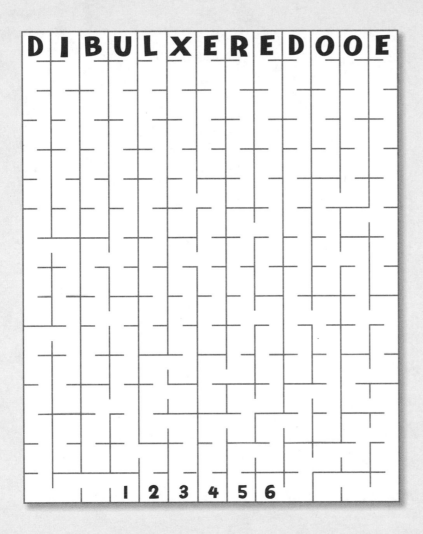

D I B U L X E R E D O O E

1 2 3 4 5 6

What does a duck wear when he gets married?

A __ __ __ __ __ __
  1 2 3 4 5 6

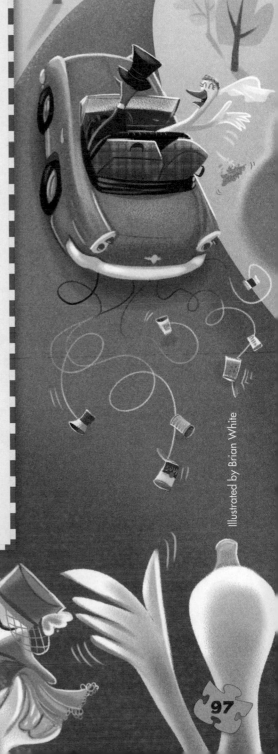

Illustrated by Brian White

Piggy Problem

The barnyard is big, and this little piggy is lost. Help him find a path to his family so he can take a nice, cool mud bath.

Illustrated by Dan McGeehan

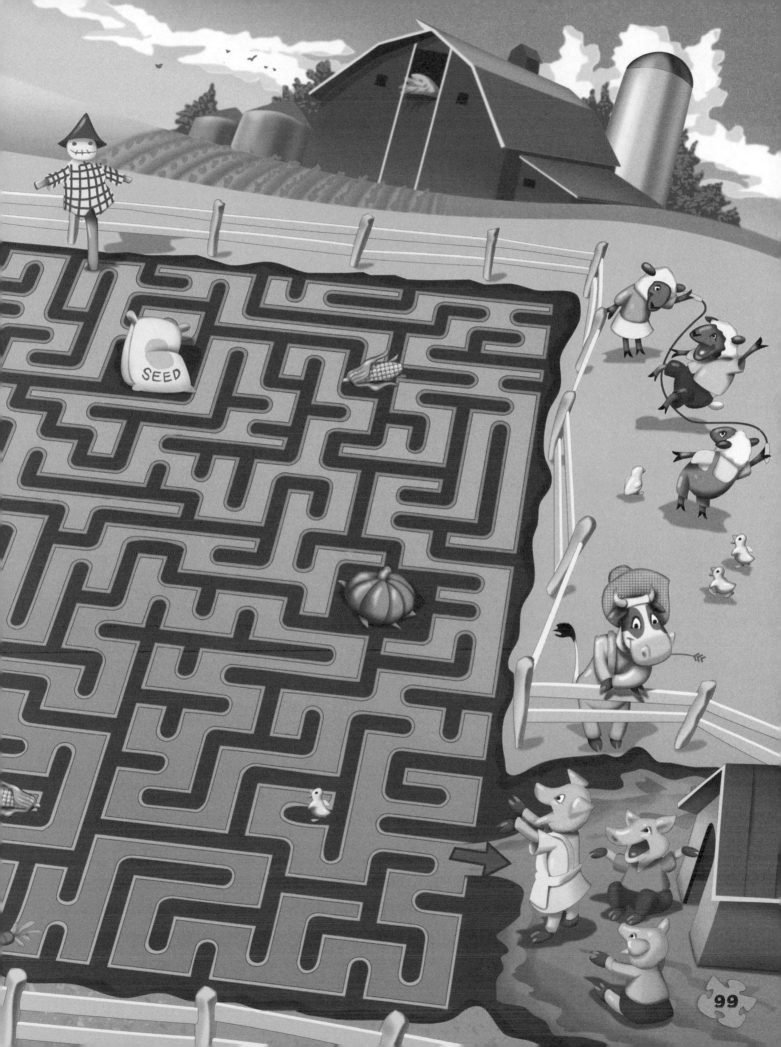

Picking Plus

Paul

Peggy

Illustrated by Doug Cushman

100

his or her clothes. Can you add up each picker's apples under each tree? Who picked the most apples?

Priscilla

Patrick

9
23
17
30

6

15
14
26
24

16
8
19
16

12
4

30
16
23
13

Illustrated by Chuck Dillon

Step by Step

No horsing around! Follow these steps to draw a horse.

1.

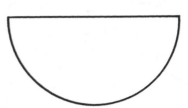

2.

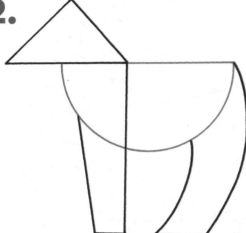

3.

4.

5.

Illustrated by Ron Zalme

Digit Does It

Someone's been picking vegetables from Farmer Fred's. Usually that would be OK, but this crook doesn't pay for what he takes. Luckily, that intrepid investigator, Inspector Digit, was driving through the country when the latest crime

FARMER FRED'S

Illustrated by Joe Boddy

was discovered. When Digit drove up, Farmer Fred ran out with a note. Can you help the inspector get ahead by deciphering the note and finding all the lettuce? The first line reads, "**Dear Inspector Digit.**"

Total Turkeys

These gobblers have been "weighting" to meet you. Can you find three turkeys whose weights total exactly **50** pounds? You will need to use one bird from each row.

41 42 14 37 17

45 12 66 39 52

16 51 1 9 23

106

A Maize Maze

It might be corny, but it's fun. Can you help Daisy and Devon find their way through the cornfield maze?

Finish

Start

Illustrated by Paul Richer

107

WIGGLE PICTURES

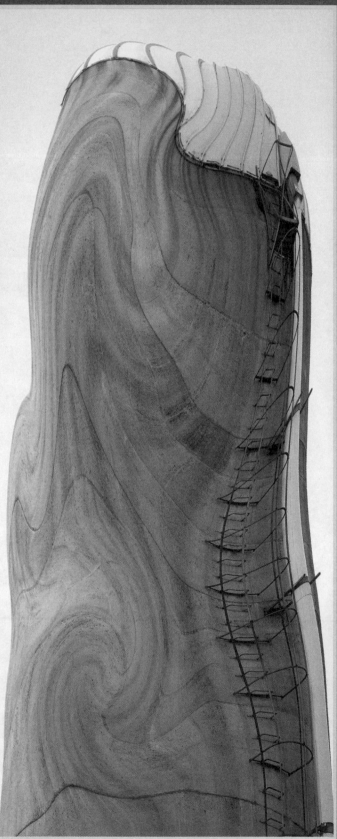

These things you might see on a farm have been twisted and turned. Can you figure out what each one is?

Giddyup!

Thirty-six horse and pony breeds from around the world are trotting through this grid. They are hidden up, down, across, backwards, and diagonally. How many can you round up?

Word List

ALBANIAN
ALTAI
APPALOOSA
ARABIAN
BANKER
BELGIAN
BLAZER
BRETON
BRUMBY
CAMPOLINA
CLYDESDALE
FOUTA
HANOVERIAN
IRISH DRAUGHT
JUTLAND
KONIK
LIPIZZAN
LOKAI
MORGAN

MUSTANG
PAINT
PALOMINO
PAMPA
PASO FINO
PINTO
QUARTER
RHINELANDER
RUSSIAN DON
SAN FRATELLO
SHIRE
TENNESSEE
WALKING
THOROUGHBRED
TORI
WALER
WALKALOOSA
YILI

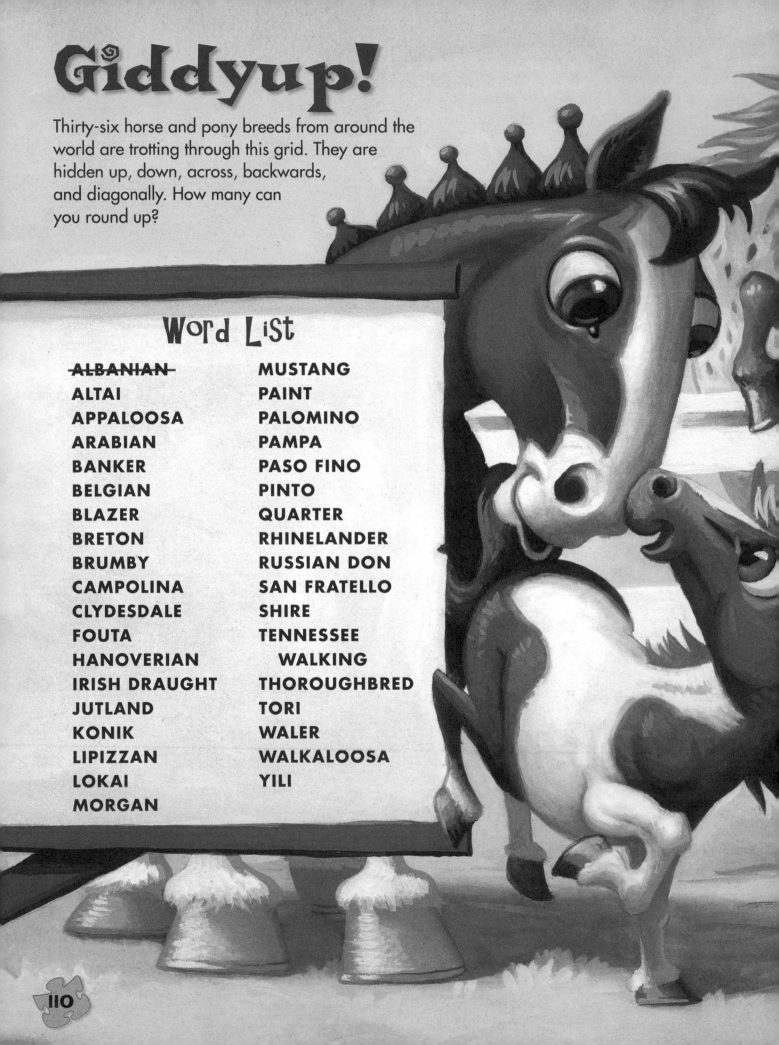

```
C L Y D E S D A L E L A O F T M
A P N A I R E V O N A H W S H G
M M U S T A N G L O K A I H O N
P P A L O M I N O Q L L P I R I
O F S R Q U A R T E R A N R O K
L F A O E I L F R O S Q N E U L
I O N Q B T T C G O R G I N D G A
N U F A N C A A F I G I N A H W
A T R I O O I I L R E K N A B E
I A A L O T N I P A M P A L R E
G P T N T O Y B P O N Y L B E E S
L D E A P P A L O O S A L N D S
E E L W A L K A L O O S A I N E
B R L I P I Z Z A N E I G H A N
W M O R G A N E K O N I K R L N
H J A N O T E R B R U M B Y T E
O I R I S H D R A U G H T P U T
A T R U S S I A N D O N E B J D
```

Down on the Farm

Farmer Brown has left bags of seed out in the middle of the field. Help him find his way through the rows to the seed.

Farm Funnies

Farmer: Are you a horse? Yea or nay?

Horse: Neighhhh!

Farmer: Then I guess you're not a horse!

. . . . .

Sara: Look at that bunch of cows.

Farmer: Not *bunch. Herd.*

Sara: Heard what?

Farmer: Of cows.

Sara: Sure, I've heard of cows.

Farmer: No! *A cow herd.*

Sara: So what? I have no secrets from cows!

. . . . .

Farmer: I had ten cows and ten horses. They stampeded, and the horses went north.

Neighbor: Where did the cows go?

Farmer: The *udder* way.

. . . . .

Knock, knock.

Who's there?

Cows go.

Cows go who?

No, cows go moo!

. . . . .

Knock, knock.

Who's there?

Goat.

Goat who?

Goat to the door and find out.

. . . . .

Teacher: Name five things that contain milk.

Pupil: Five cows.

. . . . .

A book never written:
The World According to Pigs
by Ima Hog

. . . .

A teacher asked her students to draw cows eating grass. One student drew a cow on the paper with no grass. The teacher asked, "Why didn't you draw any grass?"

The student replied, "The cow ate it all!"

Illustrated by Dan McGeehan

113

Hidden Pictures®
Eggs for Breakfast

Can you find these 12 hidden objects in this henhouse?

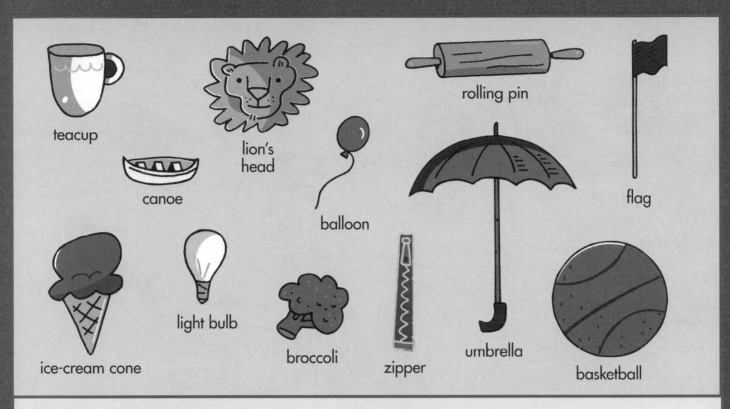

teacup

lion's head

canoe

balloon

rolling pin

flag

light bulb

ice-cream cone

broccoli

zipper

umbrella

basketball

Dot to Dot

Connect the dots from 1 to 30 to see another farm animal.

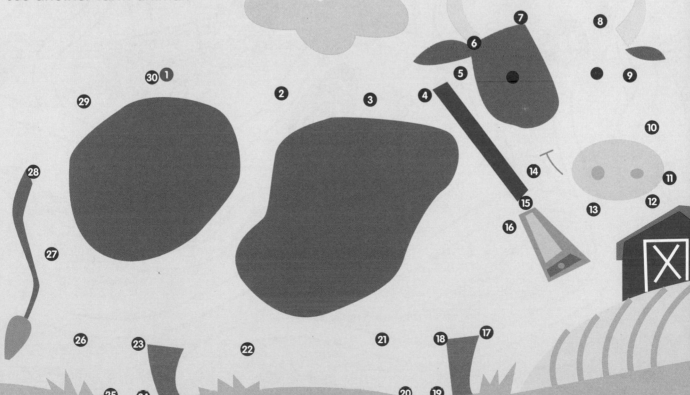

Illustrated by Dave Klug

Udderly Lost!

START

FINISH

117

Illustrated by Ron Zalme

Fruit Q's

Food with "A Peel"

Here are four closeup pictures of fruit. Can you guess what each one is?

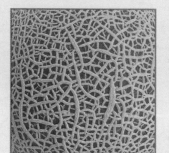

Fruit or Not?

Each pair of words has one fruit and one faker. Circle the fruits.

Pawpaw or **Seesaw?**

Armadillo or **Tamarillo** ?

Breadfruit or **Butterfruit?**

Kumquat or **Whatnot?**

Pomelo or **Pueblo?**

Snugly or **Ugli?**

Apple Picking

Miss Crisp was in the orchard picking apples. Help her get back home to make more pies!

Start

Finish

118

Illustrated by Mike Moran

Fruity Phrases

A **fruit** is hidden in the letters of each sentence. Find **orange** in the first one. Then find a different fruit in each of the others.

Is it chocolate or angel food cake?

No one can ban a nation.

Pile money up high.

Wear a cap, please.

I tied rope around the fence.

A New Fruit

Scientists are always making new fruits. For example, if you combine a **plum** and an **apricot**, you get a **pluot**. Suppose they tried to combine a strawberry and a pineapple. Draw a picture of a **strawbapple** here.

Melon Match

There are two watermelon slices that match. Can you find them?

Cubic Confusion

The shape below can be folded into a cube. The seven cubes above the blank spaces are different views of that cube. Which letter is unseen at the bottom of each cube? When you fill in the blanks with the proper letter, you should find the answer to the riddle.

What tools did the Three Little Pigs use to build their houses?

Illustrated by Joe Turowski

120

Barn Bamboozles

To solve the riddle, cross out all the pairs of matching letters. Then write the remaining letters in order in the spaces below. Don't get bamboozled!

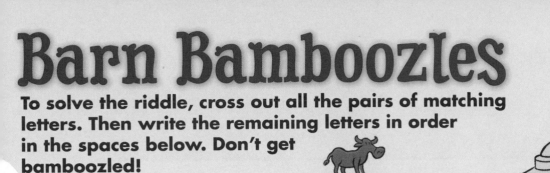

BB	NN	IT	SS	IS
PA	LL	TT	GG	ST
MM	VV	UR	DD	EB
HH	XX	OO	ED	FF
TI	ZZ	EE	QQ	ME

What did the farmer say to the cows at night?

___ ___ ___ ___ ___ ___ ___ ___ ___ ___

___ ___ ___ ___ ___ ___ ___ !

Can you find the hidden objects? When you finish, you can color in the rest of the scene.

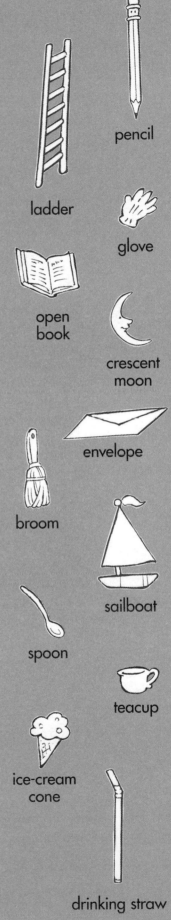

ladder

pencil

glove

open book

crescent moon

envelope

broom

sailboat

spoon

teacup

ice-cream cone

drinking straw

Tic Tac Row

Each of these birds has something in common with the other two birds in the same row. For example, in the top row across, each bird is blue. Look at the other rows across, down, and diagonally. Can you tell what's alike in each row?

RODEO ROUNDUP

Unscramble all the Wild West words and you'll be a true champion!

1. salos
2. tobos
3. charn
4. reset
5. nowag
6. hondwac
7. dedals
8. gorpin
9. cornob
10. crabebak
11. teltac
12. bananand

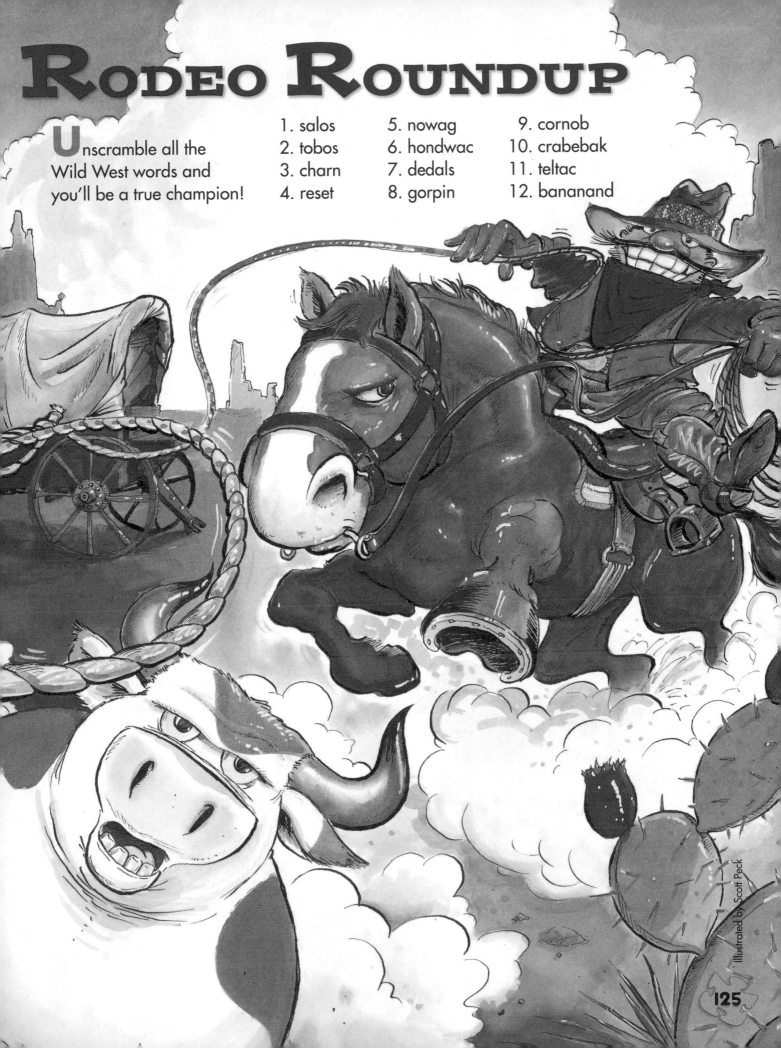

Illustrated by Scott Peck

What's Growing On?

They have their own food group—and now they have their very own puzzle! Forty-six kinds of fruits and vegetables are hiding in this grid. Look for them up, down, across, backwards, and diagonally. Can you find them all?

Word List

APRICOT

ARTICHOKE

ASPARAGUS

AVOCADO

BANANA

BEAN

BEET

BLUEBERRY

BROCCOLI

CABBAGE

CARROT

CAULIFLOWER

CHERRY

COCONUT

COLLARD GREENS

CORN

CRANBERRY

CUCUMBER

EGGPLANT

GRAPE

GUAVA

KALE

LEMON

LIME

MANGO

MUSHROOM

NECTARINE

OKRA

ONION

ORANGE

PARSNIP

PEACH

PEAR

PEPPER

PINEAPPLE

PLUM

POTATO

PUMPKIN

RADISH

SPINACH

SWISS CHARD

STRAWBERRY

TOMATO

UGLI FRUIT

WATERMELON

YAM

```
S P G B N Y C R A N B E R R Y B T P
Q E E U G L I F R U I T G R L P E S
J A O T U N O C O C W X A U O X E T
N C K C C U C U M B E R E T M M B R
L H R S P I N A C H M B A U U T R A
E P A R S N I P G G E T R E L P O W
M P N I K P M U P R O O Y E P C C B
O S N E E R G D R A L L O C L I O E
N P Y W H D A Y G U P E G N A R R R
I B A N A N A D T O M A T O S P L R
O J M E K O H C I T R A M U H A I Y
N E C T A R I N E S U R G R A P E T
S W I S S C H A R D H A V O C A D O
S A Y I H O W A T E R M E L O N E R
P I N E A P P L E A J C O R N M O R
T F R V L R E P P E P E Q E I G K A
L R A M L M U S H R O O M L N E T C
Y U C A B B A G E G G P L A N T G J
G R E W O L F I L U A C M K G K E Y
```

127

Cock-a-Doodle

Each clue describes a word that contains the letters OO.
Figure out the words and write them in the blanks.

1. Object in the night sky

<u>M</u> O O <u>N</u>

2. Thread holder

__ __ O O __

3. A type of bird

__ O O __ __

4. A type of dog

__ O O __ __ __

5. Opposite of rough

__ __ O O __ __

6. A shade of purple-red

__ __ __ O O __

7. Something you put in your hair

__ __ __ __ __ O O

8. A shallow body of water

__ __ __ O O __

9. Plant that pandas eat

__ __ __ __ O O

10. Animal that says "cock-a-doodle-doo"

__ O O __ __ __

128

Hidden Pictures®
Making a Splash

Illustrated by Ron Lieser

fish

hammer

nail

teacup

mitten

candle

2 buttons

envelope

heart

saw

pencil

ladle

129

EGGSCRUCIATING

Don't be chicken. Gather up all the clues you need to decode these riddles. Each colored egg stands for the capital letter on the egg box. Match the eggs with the letters to solve the code.

A B C D E

F G H I J

K L M N O

P Q R S T

U V W X

Y Z

1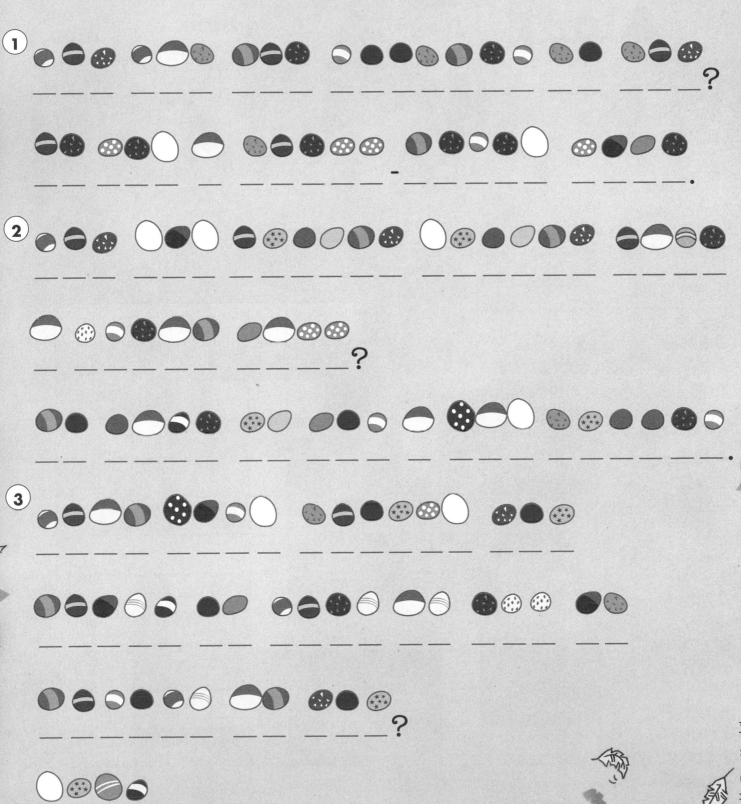

Moovin' Along

Moo.

Moo.

Get a "moove" on! Eighteen cow words are listed here. Use the number of letters in each word to help you figure out where they fit in the grid. We filled in one to get you started.

3 letters
COW
CUD
MOO

4 letters
BULL
~~CALF~~
HERD
MILK

5 letters
DAIRY
STEER
UDDER

6 letters
BOVINE
CATTLE
HEIFER
JERSEY
MANURE

8 letters
HOLSTEIN
LONGHORN
YEARLING

C
A L F

Illustrated by David Opie

Answers

5 Moo-ve It Along

Buck: Cowly
Jeannie: Cuddles
Roy: Munch
Sasha: Ferdie
Tex: Moosic

10–11 Pumpkin Patch

13 Tic Tac Row

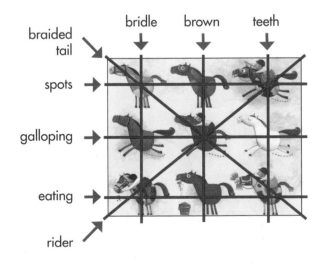

16–17 Come and Get It!

What do cowboys put on their pancakes?
MAPLE STIRRUP

6–7 Sheep-Shearing Season

12 Roundabout

Why did the chicken cross the water park?
TO GET TO THE OTHER SLIDE

14 Word for Words Basketball

1. BAT
2. TEA
3. ASK
4. BASE
5. TALL
6. SALT
7. BAKE
8. LATE
9. BEST
10. LAKE
11. EAST
12. SKATE
13. LEAST
14. STABLE
15. BALLET

15 Farm Fresh

133

Answers

18 Good Morning

19 Crop Circles

20–21 Veggie Q's

To Market, to Market

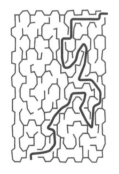

Veggies or Not?

Kale
Swiss Chard
Fennel
Okra
Jalapeño
Kohlrabi

Hidden Veggies

Please try a marshmallow.
Could this be any sillier?
This décor needs to be updated.
An antelope ambled by.
That bee tried to sting me!

Vegetable Soup

Carrot
Eggplant
Mushroom
Pumpkin

Match Up

22 Horseplay

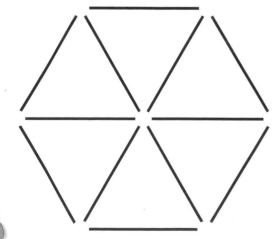

23 Hop To It!

Objects that start
with the letter *P*:
Peanuts
Peas
Pillows
Pumpkin
Pickles
Pineapples
Peacocks
Pizzas
Pencils
Presents
Pear
32 JUGGLED OBJECTS

26–27 Swing Your Partner

28 Box Drops

1. WHAT DO YOU CALL A PIG THAT DOES KARATE?

   A PORK CHOP

2. WHAT IS A COW'S FAVORITE PAINTING?

   MOONA LISA

29 Escape Goat

30–31 Digit Does It

Dear Inspector Digit,
I flew the coop, so the yolk's on you. I managed to hide 29 eggs after I hatched this plan. You'll have to scramble to find them all.

Al Bumen

32 Hamming It Up

1. HAMMER
2. HAMSTER
3. HAMMERHEAD
4. SHAMPOO
5. HAMPER
6. HAMMOCK
7. SHAMROCK
8. GRAHAM
9. ABRAHAM
10. HAMSTRING
11. HAMBURGER
12. NEW HAMPSHIRE

33 The Plot Thickens

Jack: peas and zinnias
Lily: lettuce and marigolds
Garrett: corn and petunias
Rosemary: squash and sunflowers

Answers

34–35 Farm Market

36–37 Wiggle Pictures

cow

goat chicken

sheep pig

horse

38 Tic Tac Row

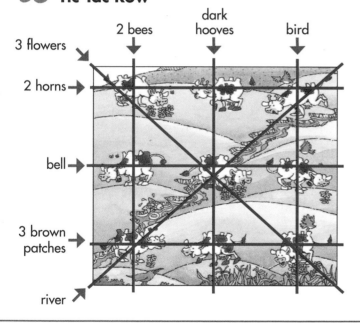

3 flowers

2 horns

bell

3 brown patches

river

2 bees

dark hooves

bird

39 Down Under

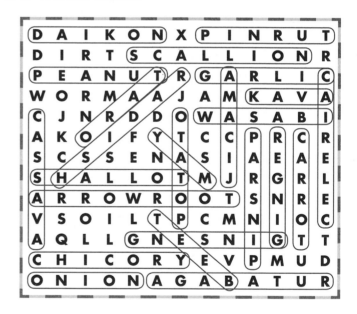

40–41 Roping Roundup

42–43 Turtle Crossing

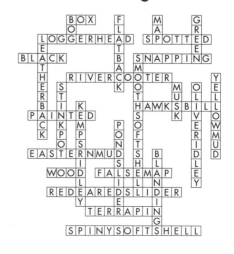

44 Planting Rows

```
      CARROTS
      COSTAR
      ROAST
      STAR
      TAR
      AT
      A
      AN
      NAG
      RANG
      ORGAN
      GROANS
      ORANGES
```

45 Tenth Time

What did the sign on the chicken coop say?
ROOST IN PEACE

46–47 Shear Me!

48–49 Double Market

52 Well, Hello!

53 Hello, Yellow!

56–57 Market Time

Answers

58–59 Wiggle Pictures

pumpkin

strawberry   watermelon

apple   grapes

orange

60 Big Machines

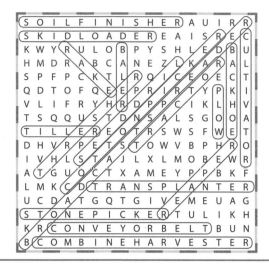

61 The Mane Route

62–63 Horsing Around

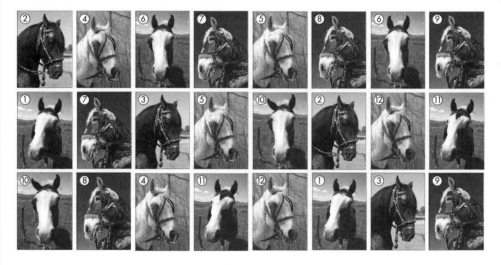

64 Ah-choo!

Where do sick cows and pigs buy their medicine?

THE FARM-ACY

65 Farm-tastic

1. 5 + 9 = 14
    C O W

2. 7 + 8 = 15
    P I G

3. 13 - 10 = 3
    C A T

4. 12 - 11 = 1
    D O G

5. 2 + 4 = 6
    R A M

66–67 Digit Does It

Dear Inspector Digit,

Had to make like a tree and leave. But I planted a few clues. Pick out two dozen pink flowers and you'll be vine. Seed you later!

Phil O'Dendron

138

68–69 Tiger's Tractor

71 Orange Zest

75 Moo-ving On By

70 Goose Crossing

Why did the goose cross the bridge?
TO SHOW HE WAS NO CHICKEN

72–73 Horse Q's

Horse or Not?

The real horses are
Appaloosa
Clydesdale
Palomino
Mustang
Arabian
Morgan

Changing Horses

Horse Talk

1. True
2. False
3. False
4. True
5. True
6. False

On Horseback

Here are some words we found.
You may have found others.

ant	rise	tan
nest	run	tea
net	rut	tease
nut	see	tee
quaint	set	ten
quest	sit	tin
rant	site	tine
rest	stain	train

Going Buggy

74 Pen Pals

77 Word for Words Dragonflies

1. DEN	5. LOAF	9. FRIES
2. DOG	6. GOLD	10. GARDEN
3. RED	7. GOLF	11. ORANGE
4. SOIL	8. FOAL	12. GASOLINE

Answers

78–79 Wiggle Pictures

carrots

broccoli · peppers

mushroom · asparagus

corn

80–81 Hay Day

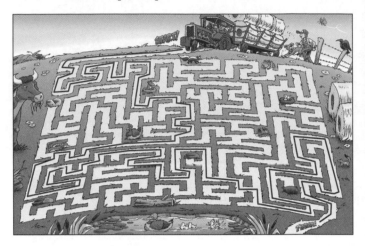

82 Fresh Picked

83 Easy as Pie!

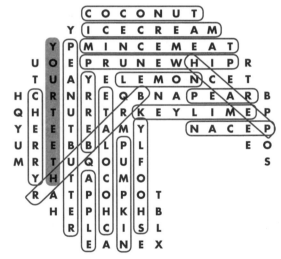

What's the best thing to put in a pie?
YOUR TEETH!

84–85 Counting Sheep

86–87 Tractor Trouble

140

Answers

88-89 Jump On In!

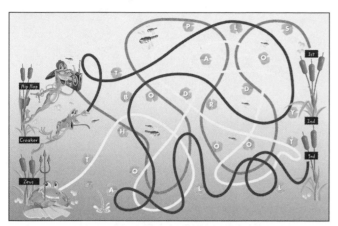

What kind of cars do frogs drive?
HOP RODS

90 Loop-the-Loop

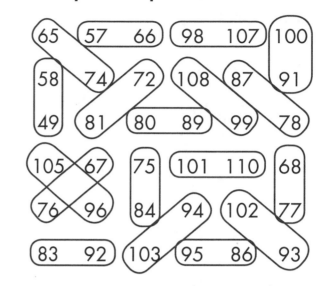

91 As Fun as a Cow?

1. As brave as A LION
2. As wise as AN OWL
3. As light as A FEATHER
4. As silly as A GOOSE
5. As solid as A ROCK
6. As sharp as A TACK
7. As clean as A WHISTLE
8. As easy as PIE
9. As fit as A FIDDLE
10. As free as A BIRD
11. As stubborn as A MULE
12. As hungry as A WOLF
13. As neat as A PIN
14. As strong as AN OX
15. As quick as A WINK
16. As straight as AN ARROW

92-93 Horse Hide

94-95 Double Dance

96 Fences and Fields

141

Answers

97 Letter Drop

What does a duck wear when he gets married?

A DUXEDO

98–99 Piggy Problem

100–101 Picking Plus

Paul: 21 + 12 + 18 + 15 + 9 + 15 + 16 + 30 = 136
Peggy: 16 + 10 + 18 + 21 + 23 + 14 + 8 + 12 + 16 = 138
Priscilla: 8 + 5 + 18 + 9 + 4 + 6 + 30 + 24 + 16 + 4 + 13 = 137
Patrick: 14 + 15 + 15 + 17 + 26 + 19 + 23 = 129
Peggy picked the most.

104–105 Digit Does It

Dear Inspector Digit,
I "seed" you coming. You've squashed my career as a garden-variety crook. "Lettuce" say I've learned my lesson. If you "carrot"all, you'll help pick up the 19 lettuce heads I dropped.

Tom Aytoe

106 Total Turkeys

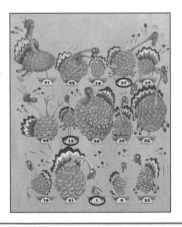

107 A Maize Maze

108–109 Wiggle Pictures

tractor

sheep   silo

rooster   hay bale

barn

142